ADDICTION TOOLS
FOR RECOVERY

ADDICTION TOOLS FOR RECOVERY

POCKET SIZE TOOLS FOR THE RECOVERING ADDICT AND ALCOHOLIC

A Step By Step Approach To Engaging And Maintaining The Recovery Process.

A HANDBOOK FOR THE RECOVERING ADDICT

Eugene A. Brown, BA, CASAC

To order additional copies of this book, contact:
Xlibris
1-888-795-4274
www.Xlibris.com
Orders@Xlibris.com
749336

CONTENTS

Introduction...ix

Welcoming the Future...xi

Chapter 1:   Getting Started...1

   Compliance and Conforming Are Not the Same....................2

   In Recovery, Always Keep the Worst Experiences Up Front ...3

   Interrupting the Addiction 3

   Traditional Gates to Recovery 3

   Addressing Basic Needs...4

   Starting a Healthy Routine...5

Chapter 2:   Pillars of Recovery......................................7

   Structure, Responsibility, Discipline, and Resolve 7

Chapter 3:   Tools for Recovery 11

   Slogans and Affirmations 12

   Self-Talk 13

   Buddy System 15

   Spirituality...16

   Problem-Solving..16

   Out of the Problem and into the Solution 17

   Budgeting 17

   Support Groups 18

   Coping Skills...19

   Journal/Diary 20

Activities

Success Stories 21

    1. Brian 21

    2. Cathy 24

    3. Angel 27

Healing and Rebuilding Relationships 30

Epilogue 31

Index 33

To my parents
Rev Eugene and Rosalee Brown
and my children
Monique, Eugene (Alex) Jr.,
and Simorrah

INTRODUCTION

Tools for Recovery opens with information about recovery and the need for the recovering person to welcome the Future. To become a person willing to follow suggestions is pivotal to engaging the recovery process. A person willing to practice new behaviors rooted in a new perception of people, places, and things. A person who practices lessons learned from past experiences firmly believing, the lesson not practiced is the lesson not learned.

Tools for Recovery explores the Traditional Pathways to the recovery community. The recovering person must interrupt their active use to engage the process of recovery.

In Chapter 1, attention is focused on the need to have basic needs met and begin addressing neglected areas of active addiction (complete Medical/Dental/Mental Health Evaluation) The recovering person is encouraged to begin adapting a new proactive attitude about their health. The recovering person must start a healthy routine as the ground zero of their recovery.

Chapter 2 opens with discussion about the Pillars of Recovery. Recovering persons must couch their recovery in a daily routine, bound in Structure, Discipline, Responsibility, and ongoing Resolve of underlying pain.

In chapter 3, Tools of Recovery are identified and discussed. Each tool is designed for quick access and application. Starting with Slogans/ Affirmations, each tool is discussed at length and easy to practice.

In Chapter 4, people provide testimonials of living enriched lives as they practice these tools on a daily basis. The recovering person is encouraged to remember the wretchedness of their addiction, while creating a new life anchored in the willingness to experience every emotion.

In Chapter 5, the recovering person is encouraged to rebuild healthy relationships, allowing space for healing and forgiving self and others as a necessary to maintaining recovery.

WELCOMING THE FUTURE

"Now that you're out of the rehab, you should have some healthy fear, it will help keep you humble."

"Now that you've completed a treatment program, all you have to do is keep going to meetings and you'll be alright."

"Once an addict, always an addict."

Well meaning professionals echo these sentiments without a shred of proof that any these statements are true. In fact, instead of instilling an attitude of excitement about creating a new chapter in their lives, people are often filled with underlying fear of the future. One can easily imagine clouds of doubt hovering over the head of the person preparing to return to his/her community.

This fear, ebbs away at any notion one can in-fact begin their new life free to engage new endeavors without being handicapped by their past. People often return to the same conditions. When the right combination of old Triggers resurface, relapse becomes a readymade option. They wonder aloud, "How did I get here?"

Recovery is an ongoing rebirth of mind, body, and spirit. Recovery is a means of reclaiming one's dignity, character, and self-respect. The world of the recovering person changes when the recovering person changes.

Essentially, to fully engage recovery one must abandon the notion that there is a proverbial recovery mountain. The idea is to buy into a whole new way of living where you continuously seek ways of self improvement.

CHAPTER 1

Getting Started

Nothing's harder to change than a made-up mind.

Getting started will require a made -up mind. Many alcoholics/addicts will start with "a made up mind" that they are unique and rules of engaging the process of recovery don't apply to them. This is a form of denial.

They may even compare themselves to other suffering addicts and decide, "I'm not as bad as those people cause they lost homes, families. I didn't get that bad." They firmly believe, "I don't have to follow the suggestions of my predecessors because I can really change any time I want." They ignore previous failed attempts to stop using on their own.

Most people who suffer from addiction/alcoholism won't make a conscious decision to stop using drugs/alcohol unless they are faced with a crisis. Some won't stop using until they reach their proverbial "rock bottom."

Rock Bottom here is when the person is experiencing a situation or circumstance (e.g. arrest, Civil/Criminal/Family Court case, disease/medical crisis, loss of employment, abandonment, homelessness, etc.)

as a direct result of their ongoing use of drugs/alcohol. Rock Bottom means, the person is not shielded from the consequences of their behavior by "well meaning" family or friends.

At any moment of active addiction the mere wretchedness of a situation will lead many addicts to a hospital or detoxification center. In a moment of clarity, many alcoholics/addicts will seek a reprieve from the pain (emotional, physical, and spiritual) and enter treatment if only for a moment.

However, as they regain greater clarity and are again confronted with the nature (guilt, shame, fears of abandonment, childhood traumas, etc) of their addiction, many quickly retreat to maladaptive behaviors with limited ways of coping with intense emotions. In recovery, one must learn to fully experience every emotion regardless of its intensity.

Compliance and Conforming Are Not the Same

People just retuning from treatment are immediately faced with the question, "what does my Certificate of Program Completion mean?" Now that I've finished the program, does that mean I'm ready to live life on life's terms. For many, in their heart of hearts the answer is a resounding "No."

"Who's gonna make sure I follow rules now that I make up my day to day experiences? Honestly, can I trust myself to follow all those suggestions people kept giving me before I left the rehab?" These are the narratives rolling in the mind of the recovering person who complied with program rules/regulations.

In recovery, one must pivot in the direction of recovery immediately upon their release from treatment. Persons in recovery can only engage full recovery upon their release from a facility. The recovering person must be willing to follow suggestions when faced with challenges of money, leisure time activities, rejection, housing, etc.

In Recovery, Always Keep the Worst Experiences Up Front

The mind of an addict operates with built-in forgetters. The addict's mind readily recalls good times and great (albeit sick) experiences. The recovering person will do well to keep their worst experiences up front as a vivid reminder of what life was like in active addiction. Treatment Centers offer the best route to recovery, as they provide a sense of balance and homeostasis.

A Made Up Mind will be absolutely necessary if the recovering person is using a detoxification facility, hospital, rehabilitation/community center or jail to start the recovery process. Many of these facilities double as shelters and treatment centers.

Interrupting the Addiction

Interrupting and ultimately stopping the addiction will be a necessary first step to fully engage in the recovery process. In addition, interrupting the addiction allows hidden problems (medical, dental, mental, and psychological) to surface and provide direction for treatment.

Traditional Gates to Recovery

Detoxification center. This is typically a medically supervised facility where a patient's withdrawal is monitored and recorded, and the patient is sent for treatment based on their individual needs. Typically, detoxification centers are linked to inpatient and outpatient services that offer the full continuum of care. Patients move from higher to lower levels of treatment intensity depending on their individual treatment needs.

Therapeutic community. This is typically a small community of recovering persons who move through a system referred to as program phases. Residents gradually move from phase 1 to reentry.

Therapeutic communities vary based on programmatic philosophy about the nature of addiction and goals of treatment. Therapeutic communities mirror the models of recovery, and their program philosophy will reflect which model of recovery they follow. Some of these models of recovery are the following: Moral Model, Disease Model, Psychological Model, Social Model, and Mental Health Model.

Hospital-based rehabilitation center. This is often used as a means of continuing care following a successful completion of the hospital detoxification program. In this setting, patients stay as inpatients for periods ranging from seven to thirty days.

Faith-based treatment centers. These facilities generally operate as therapeutic communities with religion at the center of treatment.

Jail/prison drug treatment programs. These facilities are located within the jail or prison. However, often the criteria for admission to these programs are limited to people who are nonviolent offenders.

Addressing Basic Needs

Addressing basic needs is essential to starting and sustaining an engagement in the recovery process. Recovering persons are encouraged to address their basic needs (food, water, and shelter) and developing needs (mental, medical, and dental health) with the same sense of urgency.

Food, water, and shelter are necessary parts to develop stability and learn to achieve balance. The recovering person needs regular meals and sleep as a prerequisite to fully engage in the recovery process.

Proactive self-care is a tool of recovery. As drugs, alcohol, etc., leave the body, underlying issues (or neglected problems) begin to surface. Having complete medical/mental/dental health evaluations is essential to maintaining abstinence from illicit drug use.

The recovering person can start and manage a healthy daily routine. The recovering person will need time to focus exclusively on starting and fully engaging the recovery process.

Starting a Healthy Routine

A healthy routine is an important tool of recovery. A routine creates boundaries, from within which, the recovering person can effectively address neglected or developing issues effectively. A routine allows for a sobering look at the wreckage of the past.

A healthy routine should allow time for adequate sleep and at least three meals daily. Additionally, a healthy routine allows for time to relax, reflect, or simply learn to use downtime to engage in healthy activities. The primary goal of a routine is to allow the recovering person to develop a sense of daily balance or homeostasis.

Additionally, a healthy routine should include designated times to engage in recovery-related activities and events. The engagement of the recovering community should be prominent in the course of a week and during the month. A healthy routine should include regular contact with the nonrecovering community to create new reference groups and healthy association with others.

A healthy routine also acts as a means of relapse prevention and maintenance of recovery process. Caveats of a routine are the new healthy relationships that develop based on the person now in recovery. Recovering persons are encouraged to get phone numbers and become willing to share information about themselves.

CHAPTER 2

Pillars of Recovery

Pillars are those structures that provide any building shape, size, and a firm means of holding something up while providing boundaries and structure. In recovery, a healthy, orderly direction is the primary goal. Pillars of recovery provide that structure from which the new life of the recovering person develops.

Structure. Structure provides the recovering person order and boundaries. A primary goal of structure is to provide a platform from which life is made manageable. A structured day has a beginning and an end. The goal is to train the body and mind to function best after a good night's sleep.

A structured day has space for work, play, and addressing developing issues. The leap from not having structure to adjusting to a daily routine can be a daunting task.

However, the therapeutic value of having structure in one's daily life is without parallel and is absolutely necessary to engage in the recovery process. This is a prevailing fact across the spectrum of recovering persons.

Responsibility. Taking full responsibility for sustaining the recovery process is the sole responsibility of the recovering person. That responsibility starts with taking responsibility for the "small" things.

In active addiction, little attention is paid to self-care (hygiene, medical issues, mental health, cleaning after using different spaces, etc.). This ongoing irresponsibility leads the person in active addiction to view these maladaptive behavior traits as normal.

The responsibility of addressing character defects is the sole responsibility of the recovering person. The recovering person must assume the responsibility of listening to others and learning the behaviors he must change. The recovering person must take responsibility for the role they play in their new associations, agreements, and disagreements alike.

In recovery, the recovering person must also be responsible for protecting their mind. It is the responsibility of the recovering person to avoid making self-deprecating statements. Recovering persons are also responsible for protecting their senses. The recovering person must monitor the information they allow to enter their mind and spirit.

Discipline. In recovery, it is essential that the recovering person learns how to go from point A to point B without being distracted or detouring to point C. Recovering persons in early recovery often have difficulties following simple instructions in part because they're so easily distracted. It's not unusual for recovering persons to have the discipline to sit, listen, or focus on anything for more than several minutes.

Many recovering persons struggle with not talking, moving, or listening to others for more than a few minutes. As the drugs leave their minds and bodies, their true level of maturity surfaces. This then becomes the person in recovery. Discipline encourages the development of personal values, like social etiquette and following rules.

Resolve. When we think of resolve, we're usually talking about settling a matter. In recovery, settling a matter is still the paramount goal in resolve—it's just not the only goal. In recovery, resolve takes on a meaning with several layers. These layers can be called the following: accept, forgive, rush out the problem, and rush into the solution on terms acceptable to the recovering person.

a. Acceptance—Resolve in recovery means accepting that people are not perfect and are therefore perfectly capable of not doing the best/right thing at all times. Resolve to accept this fact.

b. Forgiveness—Resolve in recovery means forgiving yourself and others for wrongs committed against you.

c. Identifying the problem and getting into the solution— Resolve in recovery means understanding the problem, learning from the problem, and focusing on the solution.

In resolve, the recovering person must accept that resolving all matters is in the recovering person's best interest in all situations. Resolutions don't mean getting everything you want but getting what you need.

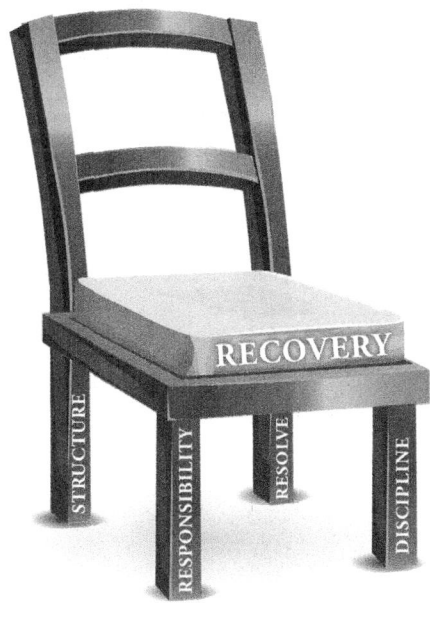

CHAPTER 3

Tools for Recovery

The primary goal of these tools is to provide a firm foundation for the recovery process. These tools should be studied and practiced. These tools can be used in every situation and circumstance of daily living.

The greatest tools of recovery lie within the recovering person themselves. The recovering person must be prepared to take an honest look at the misery or wreckage of the past. The recovering person must maintain an attitude of humility as a permanent student of life.

The recovering person must resist the illusion of success where there is no comparable work. The recovering person must resist taking the shortcut in most situations. Taking shortcuts in life often makes a person miss the fine points that ensure success in an ongoing journey. The recovering person accepts that life will invariably require a life raft.

"Tools for Recovery" provides those life rafts needed when times are most challenging. In difficult moments, it may not be easy to remember eloquent words of a well-wisher. One of those life rafts or tools is slogans. Slogans should be practiced (preferably in cadence style) and remembered, adding new meaning to life's challenges.

Slogans and Affirmations

For many recovering persons, slogans and empowering statements can be instrumental in helping to change entrenched behavior patterns. Statements should be challenging yet simple in its application. Many recovering persons have become empowered by placing statements or slogans in strategic places in the home and close living space.

"Forget the experience. Grab the lesson."

Resist the temptation to stay in any experience too long after the experience. In every experience, there is a lesson to be learned. The recovering person must identify the lessons and practice them ad nauseam.

"A lesson not practiced is a lesson not learned."

New lessons must be practiced for them to become habits. This will definitely involve behavior changes that demonstrate the new lesson in real time. It is generally believed that any behavior done consistently for ninety days or more can be habitual. This is an action that can only be done by the person in recovery, as they are the authors of the lessons they learned.

"A setback is not a go-back."

Recovery on many levels can only be compared to being reborn with a new vision, a sense of urgency, and a hope for a better tomorrow. Recovery means facing life on life's terms and experiencing the hills, valleys, setbacks, disappointments, joys, love, and even dreams deferred. However, for the person in recovery to be set back by an unplanned circumstance or situation never means going back to the beginning. There are lessons to be learned from every situation, with the greatest lessons coming at a cost.

"True character is not what you do when everybody's looking. True character is what you do when nobody's looking."

It is important for the recovering person to practice their new behaviors on a consistent basis. A primary goal is to internalize these new behavior patterns. The most important part of this tool is that the recovering person learns to place the greatest value on the fact that he/she is looking.

Self-Talk

The recovering person needs to avoid making disparaging remarks about themselves. Learning the power of the tongue is a primary goal. All self-talk should be encouraging and supportive. The recovering person needs to be their biggest fan.

"Finish strong."

Statements such as "Finish strong" can be helpful to encourage the recovering person not to give up. Statements, when placed at strategic locations around the house, serve to encourage the recovering person on a regular basis. Many recovering persons have the tendency to slack off when they believe their nearing the end of anything. "Finish strong" is a statement designed to encourage the recovering person to finish any project strong.

"Struggle breeds strength."

Many recovering persons struggle with developing and sticking to a healthy routine. Some struggle with conflicting needs and struggle to identify their priorities. Still others become frustrated with the pace or outcome of their efforts and are at high risk of relapse by default.

Remember growth is uncomfortable. The greater the struggle the stronger you will be in the outcome.

"Attitude will determine altitude."

It is generally accepted that in the recovering community, there is what's often referred to as the 20-60-20 rule. Essentially, for the recovering person, attitude is everything—how great is the recovering person's sense of urgency to engage and maintain recovery.

That means 20 percent of the recovery population has no interest in recovery. These are usually people who have been mandated to treatment to avoid jail or other uncomfortable consequences.

These people are the most visible in any recovery community. They will advertise their maladaptive behavior patterns as personal trophies—won in the battlefield of a dysfunctional family or a poverty-stricken neighborhood. This particular population can be best at recruiting others.

Sixty percent of the recovering population are not fully engaging the recovery process, nor are they consistently rejecting the recovery process. Many of this population struggle to keep one foot on both sides while being pulled in different directions.

These are usually recovering persons who lack a sense of self-efficacy, confidence, and leadership. This population is quick to display their mixed feelings. Individuals in this group often follow whom they perceive to have power at the moment. They aren't necessarily committed to people not in recovery, nor are they committed to people in recovery.

The remaining 20 percent of the recovering population are often referred to as the no-matter-what people. These people put nothing in front of their recovery. These recovering persons have fully accepted all the tenets (healing, forgiveness, acceptance, gratitude, humility, rebirth, etc.) of the recovery process.

They view themselves as a student of life for life. They have an optimistic attitude about recovery, believing that one day of sobriety is better than a hundred days of being high. They have regained their pride, dignity, and self-respect. All persons fully into recovery are striving to join this group of recovering persons.

Not everything that is faced will be changed, but
nothing can be changed unless it's faced.

—James Baldwin

Many recovering persons fear that some of the wreckage of their past will be with them for life. They suspect the existence of an underlying problem as a direct result of reckless behavior. The now-recovering person may remember when and where they placed themselves at risk. In active addiction, there's little concern for health or well-being. Now, the recovering person must face their fear of learning what the wreckage of their past experiences is.

At times, they wake up to learn they will now suffer a particular disease or problem for the rest of their lives. This alone can send many recovering persons back to active addiction simply by the overwhelming feelings of guilt and shame. However, for the recovering person, this can be further motivation to make healthy behavioral changes suited to a new life of recovery.

Buddy System

For many recovering persons, visiting new places where they may be expected to reveal information about themselves can be intimidating.

This is where finding a supportive buddy to travel with or lead as a mentor is paramount. Ideally, this buddy shares a mutual respect for recovery and therefore understands the urgency in connecting to community support (medical health, mental health, dental health, etc.).

A buddy helps to acclimate the recovering person to the rigors (developing a healthy routine, keeping commitments, etc.) of recovery. At times, it may be necessary for the recovering person to allow a friend to take them to support groups regularly for the first thirty days.

The buddy system also helps persons confront specific triggers (e.g., money, spare time) directly. A buddy can be instrumental in helping the recovering person become desensitized to specific triggers. This is a primary reason why most recovering persons are encouraged to identify a buddy (a.k.a. sponsor, helper, guide, etc.) early in the recovery process.

Ideally, the buddy should share recovery values to help the recovering person connect to the recovery community. The recovering person needs to connect to a new reference group to develop a better self-image. Enhancing the social network provides a framework for new, healthy relationships.

Spirituality

In recovery, spirituality simply means the source that brings peace. Many recovering persons become racked with guilt and shame when they reflect on things they've done while engaged in drug activity.

Many will confuse spirituality with religion. To be clear, in recovery, the primary goal is to identify a power greater than self. Contrary to popular community support-group thinking, here the idea is a power that calms and empowers the believer. This power must be greater than the individual for it to have the calming impact sought in recovery.

Problem-Solving

Many times, problems appear larger simply because of our perception and situation. Remember, everything looks larger when viewed from lying on the floor (metaphor for being down on your luck at that time). However, as you slowly improve, so does your perception of the problem. To start, view your problems as challenges to be conquered as opposed to insurmountable odds to overcome. How you view your problems will determine the effectiveness of your solution.

Here is the plan:

Step 1. Separate the problems.

Step 2. Prioritize the problems in order of importance.

Step 3. Focus 100 percent on each problem by order of importance.

Out of the Problem and into the Solution

Many recovering persons have made an art of circling a problem. In recovery, the goal is to learn from problems and give equal or greater attention to the solution. The idea being, the quicker the resolution of one problem, the sooner the recovering person can move to the next problem.

Budgeting

In recovery, learning to budget one's finances and pay one's bills is a valuable tool in maintaining recovery. In active addiction, money is spent recklessly, fueled by emotions. In recovery, budgeting is a relapse prevention tool geared to keep the recovering person capable of managing their personal affairs.

Learning to resist the temptation to spend money recklessly becomes a challenge that builds discipline and character. Budgeting also helps the recovering person resist channeling maladaptive behaviors to related process addictions (e.g., shopping, gambling). Budgeting is a valuable tool of recovery that supports maintaining the recovery process.

Budgeting can be intimidating to the person who has never made / lived by a budget. However, budgeting will directly impact one's credit, one's available funds, and one's ability to live within one's means. This is a particularly daunting task to the person who has difficulty paying bills.

Here's the plan:

Step 1. Separate bills.

Step 2. List in them order of importance.

Step 3. Focus 100 percent on each bill.

Support Groups

In recovery, support groups serve the dual purpose of providing the recovering person emotional support and providing group identification. Ideally, a support group ultimately includes family, friends, and activities. Each of these components serves distinct roles in the recovery process with inherent benefits.

Many recovering persons experience a sense of loneness in the early days of their recovery. The support group helps drive home the message, "You are neither unique nor alone." This new group affiliation often becomes a driving force to engage in the recovery process. Recovering persons are empowered by their group membership, and for many, their support group becomes the primary source of emotional support.

Essentially, group members become an important source of emotional support and a strong influence, promoting the engagement of the recovery process. The group imparts the message, "We support you and believe you too can stop."

However, other parts of the support network are equally important. They are made up of family, friends, and activities.

Family support is helpful. The recovering person will benefit from identifying supportive family members. There's no doubt addiction is a family disease, and as such, all family members may not be supportive in the beginning of the recovery process. However, as the recovering person improves, so does his or her family and family relations.

In some instances, family members may not welcome the recovering person making healthy changes. This is often due to the family having grown tired of broken promises to change by the recovering person. Additionally, in some instances, family members benefit from the insanity of the recovering person and are reluctant to give up ill-gotten gains (e.g., family member as proxy for pension checks, SSI, etc.)

Furthermore, it's equally important not to associate with nonsupportive family members. Addiction negatively impacts the family as a unit. Recovery, on the other hand, allows everyone to heal.

Activity is essential to any support network. This can be low-level activities, such as playing cards or dominoes. It can be high-level activities (e.g., swimming, basketball), which require better health and stamina. The goal is to engage in some healthy leisure-time activities with others.

Coping Skills

> When I was a boy, I thought as a boy, but when I
> became a man, I put away childish things.

> The difference between a man and a boy
> is that a man acts, a boy reacts.

The challenge of learning new ways to cope with reality becomes the most evident example of the recovery process.

Some of these coping skills will include but are not limited to the following:

a. Avoid high-risk situations alone.
b. Take care of your body, mind, and spirit.
c. Be proactive in all your affairs. Procrastination is never a suitable option.
d. Don't wait till something happens before acting in your interest.
e. Ask for help when you don't have the answer.
f. Stay in the moment. Resist the temptation to act in the future.

Learning new coping skills is ongoing since situations and circumstances vary in urgency and emotional intensity. However, practicing new coping skills is essential to learning new coping skills. Remember, the lesson not practiced is the lesson not learned.

Journal/Diary

Many recovering persons may choose to record their progress, feelings, and coping skills, among other things. This is when a journal works best.

A journal enables many recovering persons to monitor their progress and note their emotional patterns. This becomes instrumental in identifying specific behaviors that act as barriers to change and engage in the recovery process. Additionally, the recovering person learns times, days, or situations where they are more at risk for relapse. Furthermore, emotional patterns come to the surface in journals. The recovering person can now watch themselves grow or continue to stagnate in the throes of recovery.

Success Stories

Brian

I was eleven years old when I was introduced to heroin by my sister's boyfriend. He told me it was a drug. Somehow, I welcomed the experiment. He never told me that sniff would worsen my cycle of depression.

He never mentioned that I would experience a horrifying, vicious cycle of addiction that would lead me to prison and countless emergency room visits from overdoses. He also didn't mention that the combination of my depression and addiction would lead to the certain death of all my dreams.

Several months earlier, my family was evicted from our private home in St. Albans, Queens. We now lived separately in Brownsville, Brooklyn, and the South Bronx. I shuffled between both places, but I lived with my father in Brooklyn.

Living in Brooklyn meant learning to fight for my personal belongings and being up front and personal with addicts. In Queens, I lived in a private house with a grapevine, an apple tree, and a pear tree in the yard. I had neighbors like Ella Fitzgerald, A. Phillip Randolph, and

James Brown. In Brooklyn, heroin addicts nodded out on my front steps, while alcoholics brazenly fought for nothing right in the streets.

From the moment I first visited the Bronx, I sought to send the message that I was from Brownsville: "Never ran, never will" (a community motto echoed by people who live in Brownsville). I remember James Brown had a new song out called "Say It Loud, I'm Black and I'm Proud." I remember being happy to learn something about myself, even though I knew nothing else. I did know I needed something to numb the painful experiences I had as a twelve-year-old boy living in Brooklyn, New York.

I started experimenting with beer and weed at twelve years old. By fifteen years old, I was skin-popping heroin to escape the harsh realities of my life.

My father lay dying of diabetes and of the cumulative effects of poor eating habits. My mother was married to a man who wore women's clothing and preyed on the boys in the neighborhood. In high school, I was experiencing raw racism and concerted efforts by specific teachers to funnel African American males deemed to be too smart to noncompetitive classes and trade schools. I felt helpless and terrified at the thought that my father would die before I could become a doctor and find a cure for diabetes.

Race, poverty, and social isolation filled my days. The roars of fire engines, police sirens, and rats chewing through the walls filled my nights. The only peace I found was in the pocket of a syringe. Finally, I graduated from an alternative high school in Harlem at twenty years old.

In my last year of high school, my claim to fame was that I always had a joint in my bag for the ride home from school. I was often invited to parties just because my classmates knew I always had weed. My school learned that I was handing out invitations to the National (Weed) Smoke-Out Day held in Central Park (NY) weeks before my graduation. School administrators refused to let me march in the graduation.

I was twenty-three years old when the dean at my college sent me a letter informing me the school would not let me graduate with a GPA of 2.0. I was in my senior year when I decided to transfer to another college rather than stop smoking weed. Unbeknownst to me was that my drug use would lead to divorce, abandonment, loss, and countless rehabilitation centers. By thirty-seven years old, I was going in and out of jails and finally going to prison.

As I waited to go to prison, I realized the only consistent aspect of my life was my absolute refusal to experience any of my feelings as they were. I had to be high or numb just to accept what life had to offer me. I never thought about the need for me to change in order for my life to change. This is when I started a relationship with God, and I strengthened this relationship while in prison.

When I was released after spending two and a half years in prison, I went home with the plan that I would never return to prison. I was truly surprised to learn that my wife no longer wanted me in her life. I slowly began to realize I didn't know this woman with whom I had two children. I found myself again needing to be numb to accept this reality. I started using cocaine to numb my pain, and within weeks, I was back in prison.

Alone in my cell, I cried as I wondered how I could subject myself to drug addiction, knowing the cycle of horror and prison. I asked myself repeatedly, "What will make me and when will I stop? Why do I have to wait for something more horrible to happen before I truly accept the fact that I must stop or face institutions, jails, and finally, death?" I found peace in my relationship with God.

Upon my release from prison, I decided I would do three things that would keep me focused: I would strengthen my relationship with God, start experiencing my feelings, and finally take off the mask. I became open to going to support groups, getting therapy for my untreated depression, and I was willing to tell another person about my fears, joys, and failures. Finally, I began to experience real freedom from the inside out.

Today, my relationship with God is my most important relationship. I welcome the opportunities life gives me to experience the good and bad alike. I use discipline, responsibility, structure, and resolve as the pillars of my ongoing rebirth in the healing and recovery process.

Cathy

My story began when I was twelve years old and I found out my parents were divorcing. I suddenly didn't know what to expect in my future. I remember wishing my parents would find a way to work things out rather than destroy the only life I knew. It was soon after that I started hanging out with the "hip kids," smoking pot and drinking beer.

Alcohol became my best friend. Somehow, I took to drinking right away. I noticed that I spoke up for myself, and people hesitated to come near me. It wasn't too long after that I started sleeping with different guys in the neighborhood. This got my parents' attention, but by now, my father was remarried, and my brother was about to be born. I was seventeen years old when I got arrested for my first DWI.

I was sent to a rehabilitation center for the first time, and a counselor told me I was an alcoholic. I didn't believe I couldn't drink alcohol anymore. By the time I was twenty-five, I found myself arrested maybe ten times for DWI. I was finally arrested for vehicular assault. I was sentenced to four years in prison on my thirtieth birthday.

I remember feeling a strange sense of being rescued as I rode the bus to the prison. In prison, I had my first seizure. At the hospital, they told me I had a liver infection, hepatitis C, and epilepsy. The doctor said I would have seizures for the rest of my life.

That night, as I sat alone in my cell, I cried as I thought, *This must be what they meant when they said I have to reach my bottom.* I was tired of jails and hospitals, having no real friends, and always gravitating to trouble, negative people, and depression. I guess this is what they meant when they said I have to get sick and tired of being sick and tired of doing the same things and getting the same results.

I woke up the next day, determined to make some changes in my life, starting with learning how to live. I realized I couldn't remember when I did productive kinds of things that would help me in the future. I lived so long doing so wrong I wasn't sure what was right or normal 'cause I couldn't remember when I might have been normal.

I started a healthy morning routine of getting up early and praying, reading, and exercising. Soon I had an afternoon and evening routine for every day of the week. I practiced this routine for the entire time I was in prison to get me in the habit of being responsible for every hour of my day.

On the day of my release, I made a promise to myself to stick to my routine no matter what. While I rode in the cab, my eyes caught sight of the liquor stores. My mind immediately began to play tricks on me about sticking to my routine and sticking to my plan of not drinking alcohol. I remember thinking, *If I don't want to live the old life, then I'll have to learn to live a new life.*

I took the cab to a Narcotics Anonymous meeting on the way home from prison to help me calm down and begin a new life. I was paroled to a ¾ residence around the corner from a men's shelter in Brooklyn known as Castle Greyskull. I would have to face my two biggest problems—alcohol and men—on a daily basis. As I unpacked my bags, negative thoughts ran through my mind (adjusting to the shelter, not drinking, getting constant visits from my parole officer, walking past liquor stores, not having any companionship for four years, trying to remember all the medications I have to take, etc.).

In the ¾ residence, I shared a room with two other women who were sent there from prison. The room reeked of cheap wine and piss. Suddenly, I didn't feel so strong, confident, or optimistic.

In fact, I remember the question, what good will it do? popping in my mind. That was the first time I noticed how easy it was for me to lose faith and give up when my odds don't look good. I dreaded the thought of going back to prison. I decided that I would try to keep my feet moving in the right direction even when my mind was going in the wrong direction. It was sort of like letting my feet lead me till my head got stronger.

I believed that if I just follow a new (healthy) routine, I could find out what I really wanted to do with my life. I thought I would start by really trying to follow the rules of parole and keep doing the simple things I did in prison (like make my bed in the morning). In my heart of hearts, I knew in prison I was able to stay focused 'cause I didn't want to get more time. I doubted I could last more than several hours on the streets.

That week, I got a home group (a term used to denote regular attendance at a specific group that meets at a specific time weekly). I started going to church and scheduled appointments with my parole officer, my medical doctor, and my new therapist. I completed an entire week doing all positive things for myself. I also started going to meetings with another woman who lived in the residence, and we would encourage each other to go every couple of days. By the end of the month, I was well on my way to clearing the fog in my mind about what to do with my life.

I slowly filled my living space with slogans and statements that I would review and practice daily. Within two years, I was graduating from college with my BA degree, working for a social service agency as a case manager, and making arrangements to smoothly transition out of the ¾ house into my own apartment. I was also coming off parole. Ironically, I noticed an underlying feeling of doom and defeat gnawing at my mind.

By now, I had a good relationship with the god of my understanding. I decided each breath would be an opportunity to strengthen my relationship with God. My relationship with my higher power is my source of peace and where I go when I want to lessen my anxiety. On the surface, I wore the face of being "too blessed to be stressed" (a common phrase among religious people).

I knew in my heart of hearts the wreckage of my past included prostitution, and despite my words, I had no way of addressing that part of my history. I thought it was simple, and all I needed to do was forget who I used to be and what I used to do. In recovery, I realized I never had a healthy relationship, so I didn't know how to be in a healthy relationship. The worst part was, I didn't know if I could be with just one person.

I decided to tell on my disease and share the problem with my support group. My peers suggested that I learn to love myself, then I'll know what I want in a relationship. At that time, I didn't appreciate their advice. Today, I am married to a very loving man who accepts me as I am and who supports my goals and aspirations.

I hang on to the slogan "A lesson not practiced is a lesson not learned," and I practice new coping skills and behaviors when I'm faced with life's problems. I still don't have all the answers, but I have the confidence I need to believe in tomorrow. I know my actions today will dictate my experiences tomorrow.

Angel

My story started when I was eight years old. I started sipping the leftover liquor people would leave when company came over to our house. My parents drank a lot and had a lot of parties. They both would drink, argue, and fall asleep.

The house was always a mess. My brothers, sisters, and I would race to rifle through our parents' pockets because they wouldn't notice any money missing. We also had to clean up the mess made by friends, so that would mean picking up their glasses. We started sipping the leftover drinks in the cups, and we would be drunk after just a few cups.

Before I knew it, I developed a taste for whiskey and started drinking on my own by thirteen years old. When I couldn't get liquor, I brought vanilla extract 'cause I remembered my mother saying it has alcohol in it. I started to notice that I actually thought about drinking almost all day. I decided to try marijuana.

Marijuana became my gateway drug to heroin. By my fourteenth birthday, I was skin-popping heroin. Now I was drinking, smoking, and injecting drugs of every sort in me. I had the secret of being an addict at fourteen years old. I started stealing and snatching pocketbooks to support my habit.

I realized I sucked at stealing really early 'cause my conscience bothered me, and I was flooded with guilt. I soon realized I was not cut out for crime. I was a full-blown addict now, and there was no way I was gonna tell my parents. I confided in the school guidance counselor, and she arranged for me to go into a rehabilitation center for adolescents.

My parents pretended to be shocked to learn I was an addict. They were more concerned about being exposed themselves than me getting help for being an addict. They allowed me to go to a rehab but accused me of bringing unwanted attention to our family. My parents refused to accept my collect calls for the whole twenty-eight days I was in the rehab.

My family welcomed me home but refused to change themselves. It was a matter of time before I was using drugs again. Now, I was using even more than I was using before I went into a rehab. I started robbing people at school to support my growing habit.

By fifteen years old, I was sent to Otisville Juvenile Center in Otisville, New York. This would be the first of many jails and institutions I would be in before my twenty-first birthday. By the time I was twenty-one years old, I was sick and tired of my life as it unfolded. I just couldn't seem to find a way out of my situation.

I was stuck in a cycle of hopelessness and helplessness. I decided to try to follow people who learned to manage their life and beat their addiction. I started going to NA and AA meetings. In the beginning, it was working, but the real me would soon show up there too, and I would stop going there. I would go back and fourth from the rehab to a meetings. Finally, I actually started following suggestions. I stopped doing it my way.

I would be going in and out of jails and hospitals till finally I was willing to do whatever was necessary to stop the madness. I had to decide to put housing behind me and go into a rehab. I had to put my life on hold to be in a therapeutic community (TC), where I would have to learn how to stay clean.

I went to a religious rehab and learned that I could change my life by improving my relationship with a god of my understanding. This was new for me, since my family never talked about God. I just didn't know who I was gonna become after this change.

I had forgotten who I was before I ever started using drugs. I forgot what I wanted to be when I grew up. As I practiced going to new places and doing new things, I was haunted by the idea that I somehow didn't deserve to be in recovery.

By now, I had a year of clean time, but I feared I would fall at any given moment because I still hadn't bought into living a different lifestyle. I wasn't using drugs, but I still had many of my drug-seeking behaviors. Finally, I met a woman and "slipped"—just to have sex.

I suffered a mild heart attack, and the doctor said I might not live the next time. I knew I had to get control of my life, or I was sure to die in my addiction. I started attending church and focusing on my relationship with the god of my understanding. I decided to not allow any excuse to be good enough to stop me from going to church and the meetings (AA and NA).

I created a healthy daily routine of going to meetings, going to the library, exercising, and going to church. I started taking advice and suggestions about learning to change the way I thought and how I went about my daily activities. Finally, I got treatment for the depression I had since my childhood.

Today, I practice recovery in all my affairs. I live a life unfettered by fears of failure, hopelessness, or helplessness. I enjoy traveling to new places and attending recovery-related venues and events.

Today, I relish in knowing I'm not alone. I have the support of a loving family, caring friends, and the omnipotent God. Today I face life on its own terms. I live to experience life and all it has to offer.

Healing and Rebuilding Relationships

Addiction is a family disease, so everyone needs space and time to heal and recover from the wreckage caused by the disease of addiction or alcoholism. Each family member was affected by the addiction/alcoholism, and each will be equally impacted by recovery. Exactly how the individual effect will manifest itself behaviorally in family members will depend on the individual and the family's level of communication. However, each member should be allowed to experience a healing period, during which time, they may or may not want to communicate with the former addict/alcoholic.

Epilogue

Recovery is living a life continuously unfolding new opportunities of rebirth. To those living in recovery, *live, live, live.*

INDEX

A

abandonment, 1, 23

abstinence, 4, 7

acceptance, 9, 14

activities

  healthy, 5, 19

  recovery-related, 5

addiction, 3–4, 17, 19, 21, 29–30

  active, ix, 3, 8, 15, 17

addicts, 21, 28

alcohol, 4, 24–25, 28

Alcoholics Anonymous (AA), 29–30

attitude, xi, 11, 13–14

B

basic needs, 4

Brown, James, 22

buddy system, 15–16

budgeting, 17–18

C

centers

  detoxification, 3

faith-based treatment, 4

hospital-based rehabilitation, 4

  rehabilitation, 4, 23–24, 28

church, 26, 30

community support, 15–16

coping skills, 19–20, 27

D

death, 21, 23

depression, 21, 24–25, 30

detoxification program, 4

discipline, ix, 8, 17, 24

drugs, 4, 8, 21, 28–29

E

emotional patterns, 20

emotional support, 18

F

Fitzgerald, Ella, 21

forgiveness, 9, 14

G

God, 23–24, 27, 29

guilt, 2, 15–16, 28

H

health
  dental, 4, 15
  medical, 15
  mental, 4, 8, 15
helplessness, 29–30
heroin, 21–22, 28
home group, 26
homeostasis, 3, 5

J

journals, 20

L

lessons, 12, 20, 27

M

maladaptive behaviors, 2, 8, 14, 17
marijuana, 28
money, 2, 16–17, 28

N

Narcotics Anonymous (NA), 25, 30

P

peace, 16, 22–23, 27
procrastination, 20

R

Randolph, A. Phillip, 21
recovering person, ix–x, 2–5, 7–9,
  11–20
recovery, 8–9, 11–12, 14–19, 27,
  29–31
  models of, 4
  pillars of, 7, 24
  tools of, 4, 11, 18
recovery process, iii, ix, 3–5, 7–8,
  11, 14, 16, 18–20, 24
relapse prevention, 5
resolve, 9
responsibility, 8, 24
routine, 5, 13, 16, 25–26

S

self-care, 4, 8
self-talk, 13
setbacks, 12
shelter, 3–4, 25
slogans, x, 11–12, 26–27
spirituality, 16
structure, 7, 24
support groups, 16, 18, 24, 27

T

treatment, 2–4, 14, 30
20-60-20 rule, 14

Printed in Great Britain
by Amazon